RHETORIC MANIAC

202 CHAOTIC POEMS

Cay

Thank you to my
dearest friends,
Ava, Clara, and Izzy

Thank you to my
loved ones
and family members

Thank you to my
former therapists
and my current therapist

Thank you to you

WARNING

Poems include topics that may trigger, such as abuse, anxiety, death, depression, self-harm, sexual assault, substance abuse, suicide, trauma, and violence.

OBSESSION

DO NOT READ

I said so

Restrain yourself from reading

Unwelcoming images,
any further

I would wish that so
on my worst and
best enemy

THE OCEAN 2.0

Crash

The waves slammed against the smooth and slippery cluster of rocks

Swoosh

If it isn't the liquified sky

A rebirth of creativity
The craft has risen
within recycled debris

Fed the blazing hoard of fire
Innocent poems devoured

Upon shame

In a passive,
aggressive
manner

Because there was nothing left,
guilt was numbed,
unfinished business

Shroom

Crashed, the corpsed surfaces

MASTERPIECES

Popularity
is not always
non-fictional

Compared to
our individuality

We create illusions
and then call them
masterpieces

How do spectators
measure a piece,
to be mastered?

ADDICTION

Cannot stop

Cannot take my runny nose
away and off my prized book

The sensation is getting
too good, too fluffy

Heart is thumping,
pulses are pumping

Reading is an addiction

Writing is a technology

A technology, I, a writer,
but not a writer,
am in fame
for insanity

Cannot talk

I'm reading and writing
like a mad human

LOUD OR QUIET

It's funny
in a weird way

You play a song,
everyone is loud

You recite a poem,
everyone is quiet

And still,
you and the world,
loud or quiet,
are united

The people listen

The people feel

Loud or quiet,
every heart is in sync,
on the same page

WHAT ARE YOU GOING TO DO

Stick your arms out
Take a look at
what's in front of you

It is your hands

Take a look at
what's beyond you

It's the future, your future
Being painted as each day dies
You can't turn around and see the colors again
You can only see what has been traced

Now, your hands
Figuratively and literally

Can transform lives
Shape the world
Build history
Do anything

But to every question
You ask yourself
There is a choice
And to every choice
There is an impact
Cause and effect
On which can leave
your fingerprints
So as the hand is

on your shoulder

Asking you

What are you going to do?

What do you want to do
What will you do
For what and who

You will change
For the better

Perhaps
For worse

Look and see, then feel

What are you gonna do

What are you going do

How many times do you need to read that
How many times do you need to hear that

Did I need to write that
Did I need to say that

For you to do something
To do something
What are you going to do

It's your last time

Now it is up to you

Fall's Winter

Love will be growing in Winter's warm heart
Laughter will be sewing through Fall's spirit

Keep me toasty during the cold
And I will tell you what has been untold

I just want to let you know
And I really do wish for you to know

That
I love you so
I really love you so

THERE WAS THIS WILL

There was this tree
that was once ours

It got demolished,
cut, well,
there was this will
that saw
different justice to make
by whom to my surprise,
had

The last word
The last will
Of the will

The destruction
divided souls
unequally
Was a war
that had
only one
warrior
to make
that
judgement

WORSE

You are the worst thing
I have encountered

You only make me feel worse

Worse, worse

So much, I can't fathom
Why you turn your insecurities
into other's suffrage for guilty pleasures

A dance I regret

Worse than worse before

JUST A LONG GOOD NIGHT

I was well prepared
Well aware of the future

The moment
Was an obvious prediction

I already had my tears
Happy and sad
Shared with you

A final hug before a machine is unplugged
A final kiss before the line goes straight
A final embrace before their real world closes

Before I exit back into Reality

I'll promise to lock the heart shape locket which holds our moments
I'll promise to take care of myself

A final breath after all words are found
A final cure of relief after the attempts
A final feeling after a comforting touch

After your spirit follows Peace

I'll be sure to remain
I'll be sure to stop crying all over you

Please tell me that this is just a good night

Just a long

Long
Long
Long

Long good night

Until I see a different morning with you
From beyond what
We humans know
The afterlife

IF I COULD GET THROUGH TO YOU

Everyone knows how
useless it is to
overthink "what if"

But if I could
get through to you

I'd reach out,
out of my bubble

A safe space
without having to
use words

Words are hard,
and love is harder

Maybe putting all
this time
and energy

Isn't worth it

Then I remember my reflection

I'M SORRY

I'm sorry
I'm sorry
I'm sorry
I'm sorry
I'm sorry
I'm sorry
I'm sorry

I'm sorry for saying sorry

Sorry

AT THE TABLE

It was that time of year to sit around the dining room table
My younger days as a child
were ever-so, slowly fading

Before my family members
took their last taste of warm, biological blood

I was never aware of the secrets that would be
taken to the grave
Same goes
to the cremator

The number of contacts,
they shortened

I am and will forever claim my closest girl-friends as sisters
Who I am beyond grateful for

I am and will be filled with joy to celebrate with those siblings
My siblings

The cool seasons may not be
as crucial as they used to be
before the idea of hatred
sawed the branches off the tree

Though throughout time
The years
You will discover and know
Who is and will be at the table

COMFORT CHARACTERS

My companion, my best friend
For as long as I can remember
More than a domesticated creature
Meets the eye

A lifelong partner
A lifetime of friendship

But that lifetime of friendship
Was considered to forcefully fade
Through a war that was only built for adults
And children like me matured too soon

A part of me taken away
Willingly so
In hopes that maybe
Dreadfully so

We will come full circle
Cross paths as comfort characters

Loss
I have experienced loss
Because of death and separation

ANYONE, ANYBODY

Anyone here?

Please send me a sign
I'm crumbling
Life's papers are cutting me mercilessly
Makes me want to punch a wall
What should I do?
I have so much to tell you
Some days I feel that
The keys
Are the only ways to leave
I want they keys to escape
Ring the bells for freedom
For the people to be proud
Proud, proud
I hope to make them proud
Anybody there?
If you're listening,
I think I'm lost
This world is suddenly foreign
What should I do?
My persona left me
Grief cannot last forever, after all
You can't look back while driving
I want them to be proud
I hope I make them proud
People say
You don't really miss it until it's gone
Until *they* are gone
Gone, gone
And I never thought that at this moment

I would need you,
I would want you,
I would miss you this much now that you're gone
I want my past
To be proud
I'll make the people proud
Please tell me that you heard me-
did anyone, anybody hear me

WHITE BOXED ROOM

The purple curtains
heavily touched
the filthy carpet floor

Only so much light of life
from the outside world
is allowed
in the white boxed room

At most,
one shade covers
while the parallel shade
is layered by those

Conserved curtains

The closet is where most secrets are held

Some come
And some go

My device stores the unsettling truths
And uncomfortable dares
of which I will present to the room

Depends on how hard
an angel will plunge down
on the Earth's surface

Let us hope that the white clouds
don't reach our level and fog up the scene

In this room,
actions become well
stained memories

Negative

Unwanted thoughts dust the keys
And the heart strings are being yanked
Time is approaching with every echo it makes
To the rugged floor to the starred ceiling

I'm trapped and can't reach
the outside world

CREATURE DIVINE

Your horrors
are my beauties

Your insecurities
are my admirations

Your qualities
are my remedies

Your imperfections
are my reasons

Why I admire
a creature
divine as you

DID WE FORGET

Did we forget
Or did we ignore

Why we wanted to do this
In the first place?

Trace back in your book
Re-read page before page

Fame is nothing more
Than an outcome

Income is no more
Than a reward

Be
Forgotten

GHOST IN MY VISION

Makes me wonder
Makes me ponder
Maybe over-thinking
about the ghost in my vision:

Will I become as divine,
as a spectre after passing?

THE LIMPING ZOMBIE AND THE CONTUSED FAIRY

Who would have thought

That a disfigured, decomposed
limping zombie from the big apple
would have the pleasure of soul binding
with a Polish contused fairy

Danced, danced, equally with her
Spun me, dearly, spun her, gently

Her temperature-less, soft hands,
could feel my carotid artery racing

Who would dare to kiss these dried lips
and this crooked-jaw folk

I mean, look at me

My many missing, chipped teeth
My melted, chopped ears
My loss of cartilage, torn nose
My expired, sunken yellow eyes
My boney, lifted cheeks
My peeling, hollow face
My thinning, messy dark brown hair
My shedding, rough skin
My wicked, molding toenails
My phalang-ed, fragmented hands
My ragged, ripped clothes
My heavy, thick accent

Her elegant tongue left me speechless

Danced, danced, off the beat with her
Dipped me, lovely, dipped her, sweetly

I have never felt so alive since my death
My senses were stirring up again with her

And still, still,
after all that

She was still here

You are the story I wish happened to me, Frankie

You and me, Eve
You and me

Returned to her backstage,
location of endless,
conscious rest

Here truths our sadly never before

When I embraced the
faded figure of her,
the fates ate my head,
so I laid her to rest

The sphere of kinetic energy vanished,
the resource she relied
on to exist spiritually

She then blended in
with the environment

Danced, danced, the limping zombie
Danced, danced, the contused fairy
Danced, danced, in front of the Earth
Danced, danced, for all that was worth

HUMANS

Humans are dying
everyday
by inhumane humans

Nevertheless,
we carry on
about our day

Living or surviving,
we have to

History repeats itself
out of cruel boredom

A break can't be caught
It's a disease after another

The yellow Sun
and blue waters
won't be gentle
this time around,
this day in age

THE INTERNET

Yin and yang,
is the internet
alerting you

How you control
humanity's
favorite toy,
for good
or for evil,
is a choice
you can't delete

Build or destroy,
with a face, or
with a mask on
The cyber planet
we call the internet

Not everyone
can live even there
in harmony

THE HEARTS

Honesty leaves and bids goodbye
You try to stop Honesty

You can't talk to the Hearts
But the Hearts can talk to you

Guilt comes creeping in your skin
You try to kill Guilt

You can't touch the Hearts
But the Hearts can touch you

The curtains continue to rage rapidly
Nothing than Wind's scream is heard

The Hearts are almost about to strangle you

Confession falls down in disgrace
You try to tame Confession

You can't admit to the Hearts
But the Hearts can admit to you

Acceptance is feared in you
You try to assure Acceptance

You can't find the Hearts
But the Hearts can find you

In some form
In some dimension

A weak figure will call

Sooner

Or later

Fate will cope with you
However Fate won't guarantee you

A life fulfilled

Hide behind your Lies
Carve around your Hopes

Shame won't hate you
Shame is emotionless

Beware

Shame will break you
Shame gives you two choices

Run

Or own

And remember
Regardless of how soulless

The Hearts know who you are
People remember their emotions
More than you yourself

Life

The life I'll never get to live
is the life
I was supposed to have
and you,
you happened to have
that life of mine,
I have dreamed

You didn't take the life,
you replaced the life,
with yourself
when it should've been me

I pray that the cards
were misplaced
and that my ultimate karma
will seize more
than just your career
but also that life

IT WAS HARD TO FORGET

It was hard to forget that I was in an old yet new place
It was as if I was here before
This place
This city of lightening
Bullets striked ideas through my mind as the new
Though familiar magic flashed

Before me

All for me

I wish I was more direct
Closer with this sky at birth
Below the bed of flowers
There was information that lied in the grave

Blood that connected my ancestors and I
I came from the hills
And the last journey
Always happily stalked me before bed

Dreams such as mine were across the globe
It was only a matter of time

When and where
was the right moment to release
the doves and the crows?

Maybe my authentic name would be erased
Dissolved in the past
The journey

The nightlife made me feel as if I was living a double life between

The dead and the living
and sometimes
the tightrope

Between ever-growing evolution from a bulb of a sprout
Ever-shrivelling tissue that transformed into nutrients

I saw the glory and I saw the dread
Though that was what made the adventure well-worth it
Or so I wish to believe today

After all

My memories stay beside me
Touching me
Talking to me
Hating me
Loving me
Even listening to me

Whether or not I wish to forget and never taste
The emotions

The experiences
Have built me to be a bruised
And scarred
And hopeful
And faithful warrior

It was hard to forget
But I am not shameful to let them live with me
For now
It is not like they are breathing with me
I believe

I declare to soak in the pounding
rain
And walk in the rainbow

THE BEHEMOTH WHO FOLLOWED YOU

Please come back
hauntingly on my chest

Did you face
the behemoth
who followed you

Write out the music
of screeching souls,
a choir in the hurricane

Did you fight
for the staff
that's rightfully yours

Redeem the bitten
animals

YOU MEAN TOO MUCH TO ME

I loved how my heart strings were tugged
You caused me to mess up on my craft

And I never make a mistake

I died to beat in sync with your heart

On a Saturday, I took you out to a restaurant past midnight
When the candles were burning low, and I had countless ideas to
present

I knew you would still love me
Even without all the gifts I shower you with

Because you told me then that
I was the best present that you had

You mean so much to me
You mean ev'rything to me

You mean too much to me

Just to see you wearin' my love
Just to see you feelin' my love

You mean so much to me
You mean the world to me

You mean too much to me

You are my most beloved blessing

You are my most valued gift of all

You deserve
ev'rything

You mean too much to me

LEARNING AND LEARNING

"I'm still learning"

It could have been 2,000

Desperation drove me insane

Independence was
my desired key
towards a somewhat
satisfied goal

I wanted to make
the people in
my life proud

Instead,
I left them
disappointed
and concerned

Concerned about
my ability
to recognize
alluring tricks
because hope
blinded me

When I thought
I could have a place
A safe haven home
To plant new seeds

Greed won all after 320 clams were washed away

Please keep your word and proceed

Clearly, you could not keep yours, fool

"It's O.K, I'm still learning, too"

TRIPPED IN LOVE

Never do I fall flat out hard for anyone,
no one, I don't

Is it their lengthy hair that flies in the breeze,
in a strike of a pose?

Glittering, gleaming golden eyes,
twinkle and sparkle
as their smile sings with the Sun

Why am I drawn to their victorious joy, this fuzz is
unlike my eerie persona

How I perspire from someone so glorious, gallant,
who I can't have

TYPICAL LOVE POEM

If I ever write
a typical love poem,
there's something blossoming
in my messy mind

I'm not seriously
in love actually,
they're a feeling that
puts me at ease,
gives me some rest

Reassurance, that is
It saddens me, though,
they'll become memories

On the bright side,
I got to keep those memories,
ones that blessed me
when they did

HAIR

Hair that drops like food coloring
in water, every strand flows

The texture of yours,
I can brush and braid
and finish you off
with a peck on the forehead

Have a moment to get lost
in the swirling eyes of yours

Lean your head back, you may,
tickle my chin with your bangs

Lean yourself in me, you may,
prickle my mouth with your beard

I will never leave
a scent greater than a memory

ENVY

Confess, I will
directly to you

Envy, I feel
when you flirt,
when you hug,
when you walk,
and when you
go into depth with others emotionally

There's nothing I can do,
you're not mine to love

When I have your attention

Forward, I will
find our moment

So I can tell you everything
Or else another bird will fly by

MARRIED AT SEVENTEEN

Sunday, March 21st, 2031
Aokigahara
Edge of Lake Saiko
10:35PM

Crime investigator in training,
Jullian Scoleri

Lunged over the rock on her stomach
Arms spread out
Motionless

Fresh blood surrounded her,
pooled on the ground
Chunks of flesh painted the nature

Police and ambulances
arrived at the scene
Where the team failed

Eleven victims in total
Three runaway suspects
to capture,
the potential culprits
The mission shifted into
a sudden hostage situation

On the loose,
two individuals
were presumed
deceased on the spot

Jullian was a step from death
Severe trauma to the spinal cord,
caused by forceful blows on the back
from a blunt object
that resulted in her
great loss of blood

To Waverly Hills Hospital,
they rushed
In hopes she would not pass along the way

On the bed,
like a still-life painting,
her body deformed
by the tremendous damage

And so

Lukasz Milligan,
partner of Jullian Scoleri

Was punctual in his arrival
when he heard the news from a friend

Her probability of surviving was slim,
the medical team reported

As always,
she lightly jokes
about her navy blue eye patch

When she lost her left eye
to a previous case,
calling herself a pirate

The little things that Lukasz
will never be over with

Her humour never fazed him
A trait he cherished
and hoped she won't grow out of
with a career such as hers

Let the hearted stay that wonderful way

Jullian made a special request to Lukasz
Her lips moved weakly
A ghostly whisper
The final wish was a proposal
A marriage proposal
Before her last breath came
Unexpectedly

Yes
We were young
Yes
We were not exactly ready
We were unprepared

No
I could not reject her wish
No
I cannot simply refuse her life

Her hope would have been unfulfilled
Her desire would become my insomnia

And so
I said
I do

From the Greek garden of his sanctuary
of towering vines
He gathered a bouquet
of Asian bleeding hearts

A thin platinum chain necklace
with turquoise sea glass
Twisted metal,
jewelry forged by his hands

Along

A single premature dandelion
Plucked from his field of weeds
Acceptance of horrific beauty
He clenched
the stem

His parents agreed
to the minor marriage
Her absent guardians
were sure to approve

In a matter of time,
forms were signed
for legal consent
The court accepted
the proposal for
it's scenario

The gentle man
did not beg his parents for a ring
He figured to earn this chapter
by sculpting one

No
No ring
Just need you

A body too fragile
Too fragile to change
into bridal attire

And so

He sewed a short angelic vail
for her to wear
A broad woven collar of cold colours
for him to wear

She tiredly gasped
at the fabrics mighty elegance
Such detail to the embroidery

The gentle man's work did not dance

It sang

Before their families
In a small white room,
smelled of antiseptic chemicals

She wanted to believe
there was a special yūrei
who guarded her life
An unknown secret guardian
when she happened to be in danger

The newly wedded wanted
to visit the hurting forest,

overflowed with roots

And so

With Jullian and Lukasz
Side by side

Jullian sprinkled petals of cherry blossoms
Lukasz provided from his sanctuary's garden

Across the lake's waters
on the opposite side,
watched as more than 200 shades of pink
were carried by the kind wind
towards the sea of trees

And that is why
they were blessed to be together
They were to be married

At seventeen

BEAUTIFUL POEM

If I ever stop,
stop beating,
stop breathing,
stop writing,
stop creating,
stop myself of what makes me,
me,
would you still want to be
the best, beautiful poem
I can possibly write

While being the amazing poems
I have written in our past,
past lives

THE OCTAGON

My dream home,
my happy place

One that I call home

An area, a region
so narrow, so wide,
I can hardly wait
for The Octagon

The history,
the people,
the life

Where the biggest things
are in the smallest boxes

Whereas the smallest things
add up so quickly
on a little island

I call home

USING A DIFFERENT COLOR

Too awkward
to go back
into the scene,
again

Guess I'll be
using a different color
to write down
my thoughts
on gifted paper

Well

I forgot my own pen

Here I am
in a different color

For now
until home

CROSS PATHS

We're states,
regions away,
but not apart

We wait,
wait impatiently
for the hour

Over and over

Coming and going

One of these
days of hardship
and friendship,
we'll cross paths
on the same airplane

TOGETHER IN THIS PLANTATION

Waltz,
for as long as we are elderly

Twirl, my beloved,
her passion never ages in my heavy eyes

Our favorite spot
leaves us from
the chaotic world

The focus
is solely on her

Us alone
and the nature we have raised
together in this plantation

She will forever be mine to plant and grow with

Ahead of Death,
Death shall not decompose
what we have left behind

CLEARLY

You're no one's property,
not mine, not ever
will your existence
be invalid

My heart has room to house you,
my lungs have love to breathe you

My arms are free to hold you,
my eyes are here to see you

Clearly

I'm yours,
so join the family
and we'll be
catching stars
we haven't touched
yet

What do you say

Let's travel

IF I EVER FALL IN LOVE

If I ever fall in love,
I'm going to trip
on the gaps of

Manhattan's
cracked
sidewalks

If I ever fall in love,
My past self
would have never
expected me to
have an impression

This long lasting

That's if I ever do

SUBMERGED

Thank you
for recovering
the remainder
of what was
my life,
my remains

I owe,
the spirit
I am,
to you

Under what was left
unspoken,
I submerged into
the blurry depths

Without thought

So I thank you
for raising my story
up for closure

Resolved
and at rest

REVIVED

It sprinkles
until it rains

It rains
until it pours

The lightning
illuminates
the pathway

The thunder
pounds on
the percussion

I am revived

I am to complete
what the storm
has to offer

The scariest light
is the brightest
to behold

ROLLING HILLS

The field is still
fueled with fear

I have fought
for a hope
we could
someday
be one

Round bullet
plunged my
sash,
and cracked
my seal
upon
my heart

You see,
my trenches
have morphed
into rolling hills

The landscape
buried a treasure
I loved

Find my
cracked seal
upon my heart
and discover
the love I've lost

THE END OF THE WORLD

Would you stuff
your fortunes
in a casket,
in an urn,
or in dirt

Will you be
remembered
as the one
with the most,
drained out heart

Are you going to die
by others' sides
or alone
when it's
the end of the world

How and where
will you be standing

TRADING CARDS

I abandoned my childhood
when I thought
I was ready

I wasn't

You gave me some trading cards
No,
you sparked the lively child in me back
So,
I can battle again
against all odds

Never too old
to be a kid

We'll have a show-down
one of these distant days

LUCKY CHARM

You're the locket
inside my phone case

Keep you close,
not out of my sight

In a region far
from my hometown,
you're here,
my lucky charm

Scare the predators,
repel the hazards,
all fear passing by

You shine with me
in the
darkest alleys

A POEM FOR YOU

In a technological society
where we can be
either brutally or
beautifully wired
by choice

Oh my my
So gorgeous
Keep it up

Keep up the wonderful writing

Beautiful poem
Beautiful piece
This is beautifully written
Nicely done

A human being
on this social,
yet lonely web,
enjoys my material,
my co-existence

I love this
This is so sweet
So sweet

You know what they say,
hope is a thing with feathers

Love this

Love it
Love the diction
Proud of you

I choose to love,
and with this much love,
this much hope,
my chronic diseases
are at bay

Thank you for the assurance

I too,
have a poem for you

And with every true word,
from me

FILTHY

You did not spill the tea, you poured, then splashed the tea

The boiling hot, flavored water
All over what does not matter
Clean the leaves up with paper towels

The scent
The invisible stain doesn't leave

To cover or remove the odor
By sprinkling greens won't do

Distaste

Already slipped from your wide mouth
You kept piling up the dirty bowls
Rambling, without recognizing
That the faucet was already running

Always has been

How dare
Could you
Backstabber
Tug the string further
You brought up another hit to the dam
Did you want the heart to drown in liquid mercury

Has the shame torn down your character

In ownership of your actions

Comments
You regret the event
Behavior
You give an apology

Suppose you are what is filthy
Someone who left you

The filth
In the mug
In your room
A rotting tea bag with no excuses

Think of the cabin

In our home that will oversee the mountains
The entirety of nature's seasons

Out of friendship
Out of love

Sisters are to cry together
You kneel by her side

On top
of the world's treasures
A dream
of found family will be shared
At the beginning
of the night

SANDFALLS

Shadowed
from forests
and mountains,
a king remains,
whose skin glowed
pure, soft bronze

No matter the sacrifice,
the position to protect
was a destiny for him

The renowned guardian, he was,
for his people's land of Sandfalls

Afar in his palace, a common lady dances among the community

Every Wednesday,
he'd pour rivers of sandfalls,
in hopes she would follow him,
to crown her in floral as his

Mighty and prestigious,
and shy and worrisome,
the king was

He learned that there was
no depth, no measurement
to predict a moment
when love was in circulation

Friendship Bracelet

I will be gifted what I receive,
because I cannot be upset
with a friendship bracelet
made entirely by hand, by you of

Turquoise Blue,
Lime Green,
Lavender Purple,
and Forest Green

Upon our Summer reunion,
in the palm of your hand,
I took the last one

Then on,
I refused to untie it
unless necessary

A bracelet that could come off,
now is tangled and knotted,
that is how close
and how crazy
I want to be with you

A bond
I will never
take off

PUBLISHED

"Imagine your book being on sale"

"What's wrong about that"

"It's in the sales section, cheap to buy"

"Your published book would be in a store"

Huh

Your published book would be in a store

ENDS MEET

Dreams suffer at night
Hope creeps at rise

At the end of the day
I have to make ends meet

And so forth,
full circle misery

SUPPRESSION

THIS ONE'S FOR YOU

This ones for the young
who still works at the same gas station
and can't keep up with the obnoxious
one bed one bathroom rent

This ones for the college undergraduate students
who's gotta face the deep debt
and shallow depths of life,
an ending to start on

This ones for the potential individuals
who's escitalopram feels little to no good
to reach for the flaming stars
before the limited dreams combust

This ones for the wild but caged kids
whose teeth are biting the bars for freedom

Day by just another day
Paycheck to tight paycheck

Are we not all that alone,
are we all not that alone

So here's a glass
This ones for you

Here's to a new generation
Here's to a new world

Cheers

GIRLY THINGS

Mace,
alarm,
taser,
spike,
in my bag,
in my possession
at all times

Broad daylight,
pitch midnight,
I have to be prepared
where I am targeted
as an object

Paranoia cannot
prevent me from
living daily life

You know,
just girly things,
you know

RATS ON EAST 55TH STREET

"Hey, girl, hey, beautiful, lemme talk to you"

I didn't turn a muscle,
no eye contact,
he took a few steps towards me,
looking at me

I kept walking without a response,
and their silence was their answer
Just a boy left looking stupid
in front of his drunken friends

No attention
for intoxicated,
low-life,
catcalling males

You hear that rustling?

Those are the rats on East 55th Street

"How you doin', baby"

All I said was sorry
like a respectful human
going home

"Hey there, white bunny"

All I did was wear white
like how clothes are worn

going to work

Not even campus security
can do
anything about
verbal sexual harassment

Get the trap out and stay back
As they are contaminated
with a contagious disease

Gloves on, take out the trash
Worse than a cockroach,
a creepy crawler
More like a creepy stalker

The rats
that only come out
when you're alone
on the streets and subways,
day or night

MY MIND IS THE ART STUDIO

I can't remember
everything I've created

I can remember
the feelings they
once gave me
when they did

Maybe I can
share you
where my
art is made

I'll have you informed,
my mind is the art studio
I utilize

And if you
don't favor it,
you'll always
have an exit
and I won't

HOMESICK

Divide the waterfalls and the tsunamis
It is nothing personal, I swear
The voices I have
Will come together as one, in time

I was sitting
On an uncomfortable, wooden rocking chair
Reciting my pages so far left me without closure
Unfinished sentences, descriptions that should be there, that I
would like to be
There

I wish the radium
That I have never tasted from my very own blood did not read So
quickly
State to state, travelling was always a new friend of mine
Until we would reach the highway's unexpected exit

What would the branch of the great generation on our tree
believe of the fierce
Movement

Their last thought before their torch blew out, they died
thinking that I was a part
Of, desperately seeking for what cannot be taken to the grave
Fortune, fortune

My former home was covered in ghost stories, horror, without
sparing a knife
Only secrets untold and that was just that

Maybe no one ever thought very highly of me, I was dressed by
loved ones to
Look like an illusion to disown, dishonor
Now I am sitting in bed, homesick
Could it be the disease's after effects or was I never really sick

To the city of life and rebirth, ironically where the riches of this
massacre of
People began

"She has no family"

My stench, smell of death brought a motion sickness, an endless
series of
Unsettling establishments

There is no cure, but treatment I will allow for my being
And I have made the choice to create my inner-peace, to dismiss
the dated
We will have a better cabin, it will be on a higher mountain with
a clean lake for tubing
We will have a cozy cabin
We will have a cabin

"PLANET EARTH"

Early years of high school
A coffee house show was held
For any talent to share with a young audience

At that coffee house show
was a student
whose name I
unfortunately
cannot recall to credit

This man performed an original poem
Titled "Planet Earth"

He said he wasn't just Africa
Or from Africa
He was Planet Earth
He was from Planet Earth

Compounds of elements we habited
We claimed, as the human species
A new perspective
Revealed itself to me
Reinforced my vision
Of an unrightful land

"You know, I was called white chocolate at school"

A male Caucasian child's words on his day of independence
A distasteful remark
To a former lifeguard co-worker of mine ago

That boy was living proof of white supremacy
That boy stenched of a rotting heart and a flooding brain
That boy drenched with toxicity

"I didn't know what just happened, I was just confused"

Just

My first experience of witnessing an oppression
Frozen, as a fire hose pinned me on the ground

The memory is blurred

May have tried to draw my fellow co-worker's attention
From the rascal

Might have gave the kid a nasty face
To leave him alone
Or waited to de-escalate the situation
For the boy to go away

Out of all
Though I wish I would have barked at him to scram

In front of the city of Concord's headquarters
Was the last time I saw him
I apologized to him
For what happened
That fourth of July firework event

"Thanks, I just didn't get it"

So this is "Planet Earth" for the colored

My friend, I hope you saved up to a thousand for your first car

ABBOT-DOWNING'S MIDDLE NAME

Mrs. Ellis clenched
my left wrist

She dragged me down
the empty hallway
that echoed

She walked so fast,
I couldn't keep
up with her

She anchored me in
an unnecessary seat,
isolated

"If you're gonna act like a kindergartener,
then you're back in kindergarten,
right where you belong"

The witch grabbed
the plastic chair and
spun me around
to face away from the TV

"You're not watching that"

How was I,
to know better than that
How was I,
to think twice before acting
As a second grader

It gets better

She wrongfully placed
me under special needs
to make a buck two
out of my weakness
for the school

Because the teachers said
that I
asked too many questions

Mother didn't justify for me,
so I was signed off to hell

I suffered injustice
in factories
designed as schools
for the following
five years

I pretended to invest myself
in their experiment,
but no freedom

No matter my efforts,
my name was
in the contract

I proved myself to be independent
and soon enough,
Mrs. Luis,
a wretched and wrecked woman,
never said a word of me again

The education system
made me a victim of
false placement

Leave my mind alone
and don't you
underestimate
the youth

As for the aftermath

I hope you're in your car
like it's another perfect day

But be unaware that my returning call
is here to haunt silently, to stay

We're both lost for words,
aren't we

I could never stop the memory,
it's been pinching me

This is my revenge,
the blackest mail

And I know what some don't know,
Abbot-Downing

Your middle name

It's Conant

Hurt another child,
and recess will be over

A JOKE

Is this day
a joke
I'm supposed to live

In crisis,
I almost try to
convince myself
that my body
isn't real

Real enough,
where as my
intrusive voices
that scare me,
I remind myself of
what are dreams
and what are nightmares

FUNHOUSE

Have I not noticed the peace
this capital city has held
all along since I was blinded
by a funhouse

Church bells were ringing more often

The downtown clock was swinging gently

Granite didn't feel as cold when I touched it

The hot chocolate tasted creamier, sweeter

I could've had a different life,
but those stories didn't occur

Only the present is
making stories as I go

WINTER'S FALL

It was me

Who aimed at the target
and fired the first arrow

Who let the bow
lose the tension

Love shrivelled up by the next phase
Leaves dried and died as I reformed

At a stranded mausoleum

I loved you then

I really loved you then

What has happened
has happened

And I won't romantically love
furthermore because I can't

PROBLEM KID

Sorry for turning
out so wrong,
I didn't want
to either

Never mean to
take my anger
and envy on you

Hope you see past me,
my ugliest,
most worst
images

Me, a problem,
problem kid,
going back and forth,
to the drawing board

SAFE FEAR

You can't,
you can't
say anything
to reflect
the uproars

The head-butting
raises my
anxiety levels,
safe fear

It's not worth it
It's not worth the energy
It'll only go to waste

There's no winner or loser
There's no way
of doing
the changing
for them

METAL MOUTH

Jaw
Jittering

Only a daydream
reassures and self-parents
the pre-pubescent

The imagination
was brought to life
to distract

The unimaginable pain
that was
to come

Comfort the youth,
while some changes are temporary

A metal mouth
is bejeweled teeth

Look poor, act rich

Sleep eventually devoured the anxiety
So the vulnerable structures morph
Shift

OLD SOUL

Mature I was
for my ripe,
tender age of childhood

Due to the
tremendous and
concerning situations

My soul aged

Older
Than usual

Than what I should be
Than what should've been

No mind of clay

deserves a life
of that kind of suffrage

Violence
domesticated
borns a soul older

VULNERABILITY

Femme fatale's
star-crossed sides

Disperse outside
the corners of
enforced limitations

Her vulnerability

To withstand
the open clear,
and the clothed midnight

Exposed

Bare beauty,
the core of
what it means
to be human

13

She was 13
on the steps
by the shore

I was 13, but
with a laptop
on the floor

Pages,
Her 13 was burned in a fireplace
And pages,
My 13 was thrown in a casket

Uneasy respiration,
forbidden artistry,
still here,
and here to stay

Did you do your poem?

As the youngest generation,
she encouraged my potential,
raised the potential I had
that she didn't get to
express

All because the generation before her
threw her potential in the ruthless flames,
and her mother
felt no remorse

Mine didn't either

Listening to Their Melodies

Did anyone ever tell you

About how
they sang

Songs that echoed
for joy and for help

Even so,
you didn't
bother listening
to their melodies

Your child
wrote songs
you didn't
think about

Never would
have known,
would you
have known?

THEY DIED

They died
Long ago

They
Who stood alone with 8.5 by 11 inch lined papers
They
Crossed through you when you forgot

Why you pursued
To be yourself in the first place

They
Called for you

They
Who stood after with dreams in a pencil
They
Thought to have been one of those

Wandering joys
Searching and discovering the ground

You thought they were living one of those absurd dreams

No one acknowledged their sparks

Not until the sparks died out

I WILL LOVE YOU SO MUCH THAT I WILL HURT YOU

I will love you so much that I will hurt you

I always knew
that I have grown thorns
from the back of my
throat

Commitment
in terms of serious love
is a life-long hassle,
I cannot obey or do

By all means

I will love you under certain conditions,
but my passions
are what I yearn for
first

200 MG OF IBUPROFEN

I don't wake up

I'm awake since
nights ago,
sunset to sunrise

And I'm falling

A throbbing headache
greets me
unkindly

200 mg of ibuprofen,
not even that
can relieve
my pains

Sure as hell won't
ease what has
already been
done

To push through
these trying days

How much more will it need?

PINKY SCARS

Above my eyelid
On my forehead

Pinky scars hold memories
Lifted memories
Engraved on my face

A close senior
Furry friend

From juvenile years
To adult years
Until a departure

Without a formal goodbye

DOMINO EFFECT

A friend, always by my side
Once will I
have a connection like this

I can lean and lean
on them, their shoulder
whenever and however long
I need to

I'm afraid, though
that I'm sharing
too much

I don't want
my side of the story
to crush them
like some sort
of domino effect

Please take me
for whenever
and however
much you wish
or remind me
of how I'm enough

SOMEDAY

I love you all
and I hope the time
that was robbed from us
will be made up
for when we see
each other again

Someday

YOU DO NOT KNOW ME

You don't know me
So leave me alone
You don't know my history

What you say doesn't define me
So
What do you know about me
You did not dare
Turn the first page
My autobiography
You don't know my life

I am fine by myself
I don't need nor want your hand to hold

I bet you didn't think that I was capable
Of breaking out
Look who's surprised

What you think about me
Isn't true

I wanna leave
I wanna be free
I don't like this cage
I don't like these chains

I want my own dream
Away from this
All this

Anywhere but this

These people
These places
These thoughts
Invading
My music

I see
Too many
Colors

I am fine by myself
But not alone

WRECKAGE

You don't have to do this,
the wreckage
that you've done

Crops became ashes,
shelters demolished,
waters polluted,
blood dyed the village

Every villager fell
to a gruesome death

Or so
that was believed

I DID THIS

I am this person today
What else is there to say
I am lost for words

Because of you
I am grateful
Thankful

You have inspired me
Made me do this

Yet the relationship fell

Originally
In your name

Now I am here
By my own name

I did this

If they thought or said
That this passion of mine
Is a disease that I have
And if that's to be true
Am I a disease?
And if that's to be true
Would you still be by my side

I want be sorry for being me
But I shouldn't apologize for being human

For crying
For writing
For expressing
For lying

So I did this

Family, I did this
Friends, I did this
Idols, I did this

I did this for some

I hope you are proud that I did this
The idea sparked from my handwriting, I did it

PLASTIC BAG OVER HEAD

The grudge
against
the urge
for a plastic bag
over head

SPIKY HEADDRESS

Risk playing with the cards
or hibernate in the cave

What gorgeous formal attire
you have prepared

It would be a shame if someone
were to throw the flower pin
up in a flame

Let the brand disperse
and we will get worse

Trash the deceased
in refrigerated trucks
to the island of Hart,
the evidence goes

An unexpected Friday, the 13th of March
Sunday the 15th arrived so,

Who was wearing the spiky headdress?
Cannot test to see if it was on you
Who was wearing the spiky headdress
Crown the next victim in the air

No one shares
Nobody cares
No one shows
Nobody knows

Who is wearing the spiky headdress?
Cannot test to see if it is on you
Who is wearing the spiky headdress
Crown the next victim in the air

Who wears the jewels
Who makes the rules

Once the system went viral,
the percussion went silent

Like a vulnerable model on the runway,
you are already next

INFLUENCE

As if I ever will

Be the influence I've needed to be

Dating back to my beginnings

MOTHER

Humanity won't help
their only Mother
in these desperate
times we've caused
her to suffer through

She drowns while we drink

She overheats while we mine

She provides us
with the resources
for our survival

Yet, we feed on greed,
stingy
as we never give back

The Earth, she is a plant
that we're ignorant with

Backs are turned
the wrong way

Neglect

SHOCK WAVE

Insult a brain
that is infected
with clinical anxiety

By claiming
the connections
weak-minded

Results in power
that can overthrow
the physique and self

An unstable
shock wave
I have experienced,
my own

GATHER

If I died
would that be
the only time
I would gather my whole family

Since 2015

I thought everyone left me,
they were suppressed from me

INSTANT REGRET

A kick
of
a chair
comes around
with instant
regret

INSOMNIA

Two hands

Tickled my hands
with their slender fingers

On my lap
Not at rest

Shuddered awake

Conscious
in between fake and real,
or was the existential experience
real mirroring real?

Insomnia slumbers through me

Leave
Me
Be

CREAM WHITE PIGEON

Glide high enough
to conquer
although low enough
to breathe

Your cream white pigeon
pierces hurricanes,
calms storms,
unites winds

All to bring international hope and bliss

Turbulence will inflict their performance

Though you know better
than to de-value
your worth,
your purpose

So why not,
let them travel around the sphere's surface

FIGHT OR FLIGHT

Stomping footsteps vibrate my stand
I'm on guard to protect my stability

In front of a battle
I refuse to face

The loud sounds that used to alert me
no longer throws off my balance

Once I came to realise
There was no choice

I had to defend myself,
and not the lion's actions,
who denned me

Fight or flight spawns my paranoia
Post
traumatic
stress
disorder
Healed, though transformed wounds

You can't
be prepared
for what and
who is to come

Get ready

LULLABY OF LITERACY

Before you go to bed,
lay down your
relentless, restless bones
and wandering mind

I may be some
voiceless voice
from the other side
of the connection
I am well aware

Though I can gift
all I have to offer,
like a lullaby of literacy,
my mother tongue taught me

If no other will love you,
or you are wrongfully disown
I will love you as my own

A CORPORATION'S VANITY

The game
is a maze
you got to play

It comes
down to your
persistence,
ownership,
and values
of your royalties
and rights

Over a corporation's vanity,
your talent belongs to you,
that is meant to accomplish
through sincerity

MOVEMENT

Be careful,
but be bold

Be visionary,
but be present

Be different,
but be true

Be the peaceful violence
or the violent peace

Movement is rare,
for the human race
has a billion minds
of its own

HURT YOURS EARS

The cryptid I
try to restrain
is being released
on purpose to
hurt your ears

No,
burst your heart,
blow your organs,
resentful additions
on my shelves

Oddities from victims,
I preserve
in pride
with my work

Did I get through
your thick skull?

No?

BURNS

The love who I will see,
until life do us part,
will bring me
comfort,
comfort that is real
in my tired eyes
and in my heart
with very little faith
in what may come
to this world of fire,
fire that burns for genocide
rather than for love

HIGH HORSES

Step on your brakes
Hop off to equal ground
Down to the Earth
Focus on my eyes

High horses are everywhere

I'm one for riding
on a unicorn with a broken horn

MIND, BODY, AND SOUL

Who darkened the thoughts in your mind
Who imprinted the curses on your body
Who tampered the purity of your soul

Whose hardened heart hurt you

Whose aggressor wanted relief
out of
the victim's grief

Remember to be sensitive,
yet cautious when fragile

Humans prey on humans
who they believe
is too kind, too open
to defend their own

Mind, body, and soul

GALACTIC AND CROSSED

A scrap of igneous debris like me,
who is incapable of providing
the beauties that generate life

Does not deserve

A treasure greater
among
classical elements
such as her

I watch her turn
in fear that
if I approach,
I will be deemed
as unworthy

Turned away,
and turned away

Between us,
we are
galactic and
crossed

Turning
and turning

And the best
I can do

Is admire her
from afar

Until the
judgmental blazes
shred us apart

FRAMES

A long time ago
I found some
empty frames
for free on the
side of the road
by a house with
an orange door

Only to store them,
lock them in the basement

Then you came in,
a special someone
who I didn't expect
to be a part of my future

We shared
many albums,
from the lucky
to the
not so lucky

I had the best partner
and the joy to be
in the biggest pictures with you

Maybe the frames
weren't just sitting
there all along

On the road,

we went

That house
was my
old home,
I miss the
orange door

FIERCE KNIGHT

The usual was what I had in mind

During our first encounter,
you were the beautiful surprise
sent from Heaven's sacred Earth

A gift that kept on giving,
you left me with a lucky flower of four lively petals

I collected your lovely wishes in an album,
and subsided my shield
in the name of affection

You did not simply crumble my walls,
but also my towered castles
from the gift that kept on giving,
and giving,
and giving,
whenever we collided

I may be a fierce knight,
but may I be a fierce knight of yours to love

MR. HERB

With this silver ring I welded
from the heat of my love
I propose to you, lady,
in marriage

Lady of the clear night,
you shall never have to walk
down the aisle alone

By your side and linked in arms,
we can be dressed in favored colors,
stand as Heaven's angels crowns us with nature

Before you and all for you,
I vow to protect you and nurture you

Change my last name
to your honorable maiden name
for you are the strength I adore

Together, the floral arbor will witness
our ability to reign over the lands
of kingdoms,
among I, your Mr. Herb

THRONES

Lady in shining shields, swords,
with these bare hands,
I've constructed shelter
for a home of our own
for a family of our own

I long to travel far with you,
though I wonder,
with these fountains that sing
of seducing spells,
with these arrangements that welcome
of ever-lasting love

May we settle down,
pamper and raise offspring
on thrones next to each other

BEAUTY MARKS

Remind me of the mixed feelings

Connecting the dots,
I questioned my sanity

For decades,
toxic behaviour
the gaslighting

This is all your fault

I don't remember that

Your health is your responsibility

Was normalised in my head
Twisted my head

Airborne torture

These beauty marks
A part of my story
But not of who I am

CROWN TO CROWN

Side by side,
we will conquer the climates

Crown to crown,
I promise to fight by you

An army of love
against weather
that may storm
upon us,
upon our home
and family

No one will hurt
you, my dearest

No one will hurt
our children

SINGLE

This is my message
to my precious,
bundle of innocence

Birthed to a shameful
and beautiful world,
I, now a father,
cradle you in my arms

You are labeled female
Identified as human

Exist to survive with
fingers and toes so tiny

I'm the only carrier

An overload of stress will,
unfortunately,
be placed upon your purity

You are not aware of today's harsh
conditions,
circumstances,
criteria,
just yet

Nevermind that,
for now,
you are safe,
we're secured in

what's left in our class

For now, you're on all fours

Lessons are to be learned, then taught, then learned, then taught
again
Those pupils push for attention, pay no mind to the laughter of
mockery

The standards will come clear,
or so they will in time

The education will,
or at least should,
expose the reality
we call humanity

Have no fear,
I'm here

I'll be one to light the torch and walk you through visuals and
voices,
pass the timeline that comes with the truths which darken our
world

For now, you're stepping into moderation

Be kind,
be nice,
but not
too much

Or else others will take
a strong advantage of you

For now, you're chasing the winds

In many societies,
you'll be

Frozen
Drowned
Electrocuted
Suffocated
Burned
Poisoned
Hanged
Sliced
Crushed
Injured

But you can
avoid these tricks

The forest of metallic skyscrapers
reflect the answers outside
when the factorial walls
and floors shift

As you mature
through the ages,
you'll notice the demands,
the supposed standards

When you
relentlessly,
restlessly,
recklessly
defend for your life,
the goal isn't to dominate,
you'll prove your survival well enough, dear

However, to the extent of a riot,
stay in an
assertive,
affirmative,
alternative stance

Because I will raise you up and on how to pick up a gun
Disperse the mist to find an escape, seek company at all times

Welcome to this crazy world and with you in it,
bring a little more light than there was before,
and I'll shine with you

THE DARK HEARTED CURSE

The off phases of
my artistry
acts as my
coping mechanisms

In order to
cast a
process
upon the
trauma,
the dark
hearted
curse I
inherited

Call me a
psychotic,
chaotic,
lunatic
in matte
lipstick
and
glossy
glasses

But I'm
not a survivor,
I'm a witness

Watching their every move,
listening to every curse word

I won't be
passive,
not after
the intentional
and triggering
pain I've
lived with

LAVENDER

The scent gifts a joyous presence
in the lavender fields, I gaze

The wind sways the
willow trees
in serenity

The wild birds sing
a lullaby
in love

Pastel violet fumes
from my lavender tea,
moisturizes and
ease my soul

Tonight, fireflies will re-bless the land,
the anxiety that haunts my nerves, and
the stress that breathes on my neck

The herb of relief
disperses my fears
in the mountain's cave

Don't come back again

DEPRESSION

PICTURE PERFECT

A picture so perfect

Can tell you everything

A picture so perfect

The polaroid looks almost

Too perfect

Resulting in a disguised mystery

CORRUPTED

I'm too mentally
corrupted for love
though I can try
to love with you

So broken that I can't sing
on the right pitches

I'm trying, I swear
I'm trying without lying

CYCLE OF EXISTENCE

You are pampered when you arrive,
pampered when you leave

You are carried to your family at birth,
carried to your resting place at death

When you are born, you are viewed by those who you start with
When you are dead, you are viewed by those who you end with

If your flesh survived the cycle of existence

Awake until a wake to not remember

HEY NEW YORK CITY,

You can come out now, its O.K, it's safe now
Let's walk together in the unsettling and the darkest night

I'm sure I'm not the first struggling artist you've met
Or the first young adult to move away for their American dream

You've accomplished numerous goals
Became the world's leader in media
Before the world, you bring forth the thunder
From your concrete veins

See, there you have abusers, we share
Who mentally, emotionally, and physically
Morph our perspective on life, forward reality

Those characters of toxic characteristics
Bet they live with you like summoned ghosts
Some are temporary contusions
Others, scars, any permanent modifications

It's normal to feel stress, to feel unworthy, to feel invalid
Like you won't ever amount to anything
Like you will never cause better change

Me too

It's alright to express your emotions
I might've only known you
For a little less than a year
And I can say that I love you

Remember when we first met
We became like pen pals after I left
Looking back, I already loved you

A few years ago since then, I didn't see the pain
Now that I'm living in the depression with you
Though, we have one another

Because tonight, you're going to sleep
And you won't be sleeping with violence
You deserve to have a choice
A chance in silence

Stay safe and be well, our glittering waves of stars.

Your New York City,

Kayla

P.S. We can talk about it more for when you come home. I made us tea.

FAILED ARTIST

A successful failed artist
and
a famous failed artist

HOPE BOX

I miss my hope box,
a cardboard box,
stored away in an unit
states from this new
second home

My hopes are formed,
only something I can
give to myself,
a gift,
no,
gifts

Not of objects or things,
but of people

Those who I love
and who love me
who exists,
as is

The box is also a plan
in case of crisis

WAS THERE EVER A DAY

Was there ever a day

When nobody questioned
Your dead silence
After you have performed
Your minor role

Was there ever a moment

Purposefully, you locked yourself in your bedroom
A sanctuary

Was there ever a memory

A verbal fish pounded your chest against your heart
Fight or flight

Was there ever a night

Closet skeletons with judging eyes would catch you
Intentionally

Was there ever a day

You did not want me to leave you with the candle burning
In the attic

SYMPTOMS OF SADNESS

Breathing, I am
Not like how I used to, though

I feel irritated, flustered, puffed up

Strangled in my fears
Drowning in my tears
Whisper softer, please

Drink my tears to stay hydrated
The laundry detergent
Looked appetizing, too

Wherever did the music go

Face is burning red
Eyes are bulging blood
Nose is leaking out

Heavy sighing
Random cries

Then someone asks you
If you are alright

My symptoms of sadness resulted in
Anger

Felt a quick burn when I started to cry
Fell down hard before a blink of an eye

Itch the previous presence of a burn
Chest was painful before blurbing mucus

Arms
Legs
Neck
Hands
Eyes
Whole
Body
Twitching

Sorrowful loss
Then anger banged from behind
Afraid to answer
So I inhaled and-

Did the tissues run out
Already
I cannot see anything

MONSTERS UNDER MY BED

Irritation is a rival
whom I befriended

Voices and appearances of beasts

The oddities roam
freely with me

Science tells
only so much truth
in regards to my shattered mentality

Listen as I'm fond of
sincere white fear

I'm experienced
being alone in the dark, the unknown
exploring alternate dimensions, the unexplained
testing gruesome killers, the unheard
of what is left
to our knowledge

And let me tell you
those aren't the monsters under my bed, dear

HYPERVENTILATION

We sigh after sigh
hyperventilation runs
calling us to pause

ICE AND GRASS

The ice that stretches,
contains unwanted discoveries

The grass that covers,
beds organisms unknowingly

To us,
a species that has evolved
to be greedy and absorbed

The Earth is our home,
our provider of resources,
yet, we explode the crust
for blood and gold

Ice and grass won't be here
for long,
same to our
destructive kind

MAINTENANCE OF MATRICULATION

I couldn't breathe
I cried uncontrollably
in front of strangers

Staff members who
didn't know me

I gave in,
popped my own bubble,
and let them
scratch the surface

My mind's surface
has a mind of its own

I'm released to go
home
to a
new home

In hopes
I'll be, feel different

MENTAL SCARRING

Closer, it seems

Their tears are
less by the night

Healed,
well enough
to walk alone

Partially recovered
from mental scarring

They're ready for
another adventure
to begin

It's time
to go
back home

THE NEWS

Humans are screaming
in concrete buildings,
trapped to starve
at night

Bodies are being carried
in plastic black bags
like trash after bombings
in daylight

Families flee for a
better sign of life

As long as we
are existing,
misery will rampage
so much that we
can't accept
the news

DIAGNOSES

Your thoughts
and prayers
are welcomed,
but the social issue
will take more
than recognition,
it'll take action

Blaming,
caging, and
hate crimes
are caused
by fear

Your race,
your ethnicity,
is not a disease

Homo sapiens
is a diagnoses

DYSTHYMIA

Mentally

Sick

Emotionally

Tired

Physically

Weak

Dysthymia

SQUARE ONE

Back around
at square one

Square two
burned more
than bridges,
but towns

The bodies of water
evaporated overnight

Left with someone else's
roof over my head,
I allowed myself
to re-live

Picked up my non-auto tuned voice
from where
I last felt confident

UGLY QUIET BATTLE

I can screw your
whole entire life

You unconsciously
know you want me

You feel like you need me
and you don't notice
that I'm an ugly quiet battle
because I'll fog out
your support system

Until then,
I'll see you if
you feel like
you need me

One more sippy sip, yes
One more huffy puff, yes

I already got you where I want you
Easy to snowball down hill, isn't it

I'm here to control your life
I'm tied to your thoughts
I feed off your thoughts

Whether you care about
yourself and your relationships,
I'm going to make you feel
so much at ease,

that it'll hurt you,
that you'll miss out
on what and who
are dearest to you

So long,
your pretty face is mine to decay

BANG! BANG!

Pause

Bang!

Death, of lifeforms
already born, is death

And death loves garbage,
and white supremacy comes
from the whitest trash

And that white trash's stench
gagged the oppressed
group of citizens
to death

No one should
have to smell it

Bang! Bang!

Nothing

Authorities did nothing,
while the children
were escaping

They almost do
nothing useful

Some became traumatized, forever shell-shocked

Some became ghosts, forever ageless and lost

The grieving cycle
isn't uncommon
Living in fear
isn't unheard of

Same with the awareness
in mental health,
but the uneducated
won't listen because
they're afraid

They're afraid to learn
non-fictional and banned books
and their own guilty history

The home of the so-called brave isn't blessed
The stolen land was never blessed to begin-

Bang.

SENSE

Nonsense makes sense
Sense makes nonsense

My words make
distorted noises,
disfigured creations

Mixed feelings
rage and cry
on the papers

Nothing makes sense
Yet,
I get a sense of chaos

VERBAL DEGREE MURDER

Phrases that tormented,
innocence,
you tore a soul

A small soul,
out of their body
without having to lay
a hand on them

Every period of the day,
your remarks echoed
in their head,
a head you made
to their living hell

Your regret and guilt
will become your
sentence to prison
for verbal degree murder

You bullied a child into killing themselves

DEATH MARCH

Governments
get distrusted
by the people,
dishonest

I care,
even if you
aim a gun
to my head

One more
finger pointing,
and we'll be sure
to have another death march

REMAIN HUMANE

Your brain is wet clay at birth,
it can be mud or a sculpture

Suppose you could oppose
If you wish to leave your zone

Peace and war

It is for the future
generations of life
and death to come

Remain, remain humane
No, do not forget to cry
No, do not forget to laugh
No, do not forget to be
Human, remain humane

We come from
different backgrounds,
so why jump to conclusions

Acknowledge and be aware of the disasters of names and
numbers
But also, be the wonders as the up and coming names and
numbers

We come from
different backgrounds,
so why jump to conclusions

Say thank you to your guardian
Make a toast with your parent
Appreciate who raised you well
even if you did it all on your own

Some are brainwashed
Some are satisfied

It kills me to hear the radio
To listen to the riots

I want the children to
run on the sidewalk
away from their friend,
not a gunshot, not a criminal,
tag-you're-it without ending up dead

People will say anything to
make themselves look good
But the children can't sleep

We're born to develop our own opinions
as we experience the world for ourselves

People refuse reality,
the wish to harass,
it's just false strength

To witness what I wanted to live for
Is gasping for air, clutching my throat

It's your choice to die in this

What you leave will be
what they are left with

What will you
live for to live with

MORE POWERFUL THAN YOU THINK

Split through
Sharp ice

Be careful of which you choose
Are you being purposeful
Or are you just playing the game

Be careful of what comes out
Are you acting truthful
Or are you just being ruthless

Once it hits
You cannot go back
And close the door
Look out for the bridges

More powerful than you think
Than you think
More hurtful than you thought
Than you thought
More inspiring than you left
Than you left
More sincere than you learned
Than you learned

You can leave them crying
You can have them dying
You can make them rising
Or you can be willing to help

Willingly

Remember
That it is your choice
It is your mouth
Remember
That words
Can be their future

NOTHING BUT RUINS

Brittle, fragile, antique

I feel sorry, useless, hopeless,
as I am nothing but ruins,
remaining in dust

I wish I could be more
than crumbling, cracking
stacks of ancient stone

Outdated, irrelevant

Far past yesterday

Compared to what we could do,
you can do more,
and have more than what we had

We're called ghosts for a reason,
because we are gone,
and technology changes with humanity

And historical ruins you are,
without your grounds,
the present day and so forth,
wouldn't have evolved
If it wasn't for you

BY THE TIME

By the time
your fear vanishes,
and is no longer troubling
the back of your mind,
you're gone mentally

And by that time,
you hallucinate
into believing that
closure is the
lonely answer

Then by this time,
without notice,
your reasons
become the values
of your truthful being

So you stay
with yourself,
with others

And by the time I leave,
without notice

I don't want to see you cry,
don't cry

Let there be closure to my decision and-

Oh

If it isn't my sister by heart

I can't imagine
Her crying pains

I'll stay around for a little more

TOO PRETTY TO DIE

Some people
chased after me

Gorgeous

I don't wish
my physical appearance
to be the last thing
everyone will
remember me by,
though I hope
my whispers will
find your ears
forever

Marvelous

Suppose it can't
be helped,
because I'm too
pretty to die,
I enlighten the pages
with anger and confusion

Such as beautiful flower

THEN THE MUSIC DIED

Whatever happened
she was their ray of sunshine
then the music died

THE SAME WAY

If I ended up falling so hard,
so hard that I shattered into

Indigustiable pieces

Would you still see me
the same way

If I was much less,
much less than a stanza in a poem
out of the book

Would you still love me
the same way

Read my poems the same way

Hear my songs the same way

If I showed you the unorganised state I lived in.
If I showed you the piles of pungent laundry on the floor.
If I showed you the months old dishes in the sink.
If I showed you the purple bags sagging below my eyes.
If I showed you the countless missing assignments.
If I showed you.

If I told you that I purposefully missed classes from no sleep.
If I told you that I had uninvited and disturbing thoughts.
If I told you that I wished I could go back to being a child.
If I told you that I stopped writing creatively from burn out.
If I told you that I mask my emotions in order to protect myself.

If I told you that.

If I told you every truth

If the human who I was before
was no longer me

If I change,
will you love me still

Because I changed,
would you love me still

The same way you loved me
When I was a ray of sunshine
When I lit up your day, your life
Without having to shadow any truth

Suppose no one will read me the same way

POINT

Can words even do anything?
What makes up my meaning?

If my words could mean anything

If I hold my writing utensil
for a little longer,
will there still
be a point
in writing

And writing
and writing
and drafting
and drafting
and revising
and revising

How many witnesses
do I need
to be,
feel
accepted
based on
what I
believe
is to be
expected

Is this little of me enough for everyone,
because I'm starved from my own self

WRITE DOWN ON PAPER

This is a poem
I would never
write down on paper

If I don't
make it to
the next morning

I didn't only fight
I've hid
I've cried
I've written
the best
I could

NAKED LIGHTBULB

I've been to
too many funerals
I've stared down at
too many gone faces

I've lost my hope
too many times
for me to count my
misfortunes and blessings

I was a naked lightbulb
in a rusted home,
where no one has lived
in since a decade

Everything still remains of
what my family left behind

Left to stop
in time,
waited to crash
for good

As I was
barely hanging on the line

Flickering out,
out,
and
out

HERE LIES

Here lies with me are the unheard promises I have kept with
sister since they have been made

Here lies little to no secrets for my book learned one of the
violent years before anyone else

Here lies the pain that twitched this corpse for months,
and was skillfully masked for years

Here lies beyond my wishes and aspirations
which did not make it past the second verse

I could speer myself,
drain the illness
down the autopsy table

Too bad the intrusive,
compelling thoughts
are wounded enough

Left to be written
Left to be read

NAMES AND NUMBERS

Label skin and money
A sign on a face

Before birth,
you are tagged
with names and numbers

Such a beautiful shame,
we say we'll make a change,
then leave the promises to rot

Not every word comes true

By names and numbers
In names and numbers
Bacteria of organisms,
are identified to make
Ooder

Phenotypes may be different
Yet we are all still human

Genotypes may be unseen
Yet we are all still alive

Now we're gonna have to live
and die with innocent screams
and cries we failed to understand

This is more than history
This is ourstory

So what do we have to say
for ourselves
When the future
finds out ourstory

We said there'd be freedom,
there'd be peace,
there'd be equality,
there'd be equity for the future
But today is already the future
And some aren't or worse,
can't feel themselves

If blood runs down,
it runs down

We have a chance
For better days
For calmer nights

We can't erase shame
But we can listen
We can learn

But holding your hand out is a choice
And a choice to lie, to trust, to rely

We have control over our hands

In today's age
You either look around
Or look down

LOSE INTEREST

Inject the chemicals,
get it over with,
mine as well lose interest
in my passions
to lose myself

ISOLATED ISLAND

Not necessarily stranded
but adjusted

A single and private home
where all colors and scents meet

Recover
my former life

Deliver me to ashes to history
which rests underneath
a region between
memories known

And to be known

Ill waters surrounding
the fenced borders
drowned the negative energy
that haunted me

Though the new roses grow here now

The land is a welcoming ward

Such a beautiful flower

To be in a life so cruel

BLACKENED

Back to square one,
a return to original soil,
deeper than the roots

The stench
didn't smell any better,
it was all too surreal

Everyone fled from me,
ended up being left aside,
cornered,
blackened

How are they to blame
for the toxicity
I have caused

The horrendous
amount of trauma
haunts a family
by the retired dock

I was hoping to arrive
with closure,
inner peace

Guess it seems
that the winds
still blow south

A PRAYER FOR SOMEONE ELSE'S DAUGHTER

Lift up my little daughter,
me to You,
encourage her and uplift
her beautiful spirit

I ask that You provide her
with healthy ways to ease her
anxiety and depression

Let yoga help her and strengthen her

Guide her on her career path
and provide many abundant opportunities
for her to succeed

Protect her and keep her in the palm
of Your hand

Thank You for her in my life
and in my daughter's life,
amen

BE AT PEACE

I have been recognized as beautiful

My presence,
my appearance,
my creations,
my worth,
beautiful

And all for what

Misery?
Insecurity?

I may never be at peace
with my beauty,
with myself,
with my life

Satisfaction is scarce,
Devastation is fierce

Still fierce as I was,
since the day I met you
for the first time again

NEED TO REMEMBER

No need to promise
I don't need to remember
why I love you, dear

DOILIES

Lace made
by hand,
crafted
carefully

Fractals
that spell
memories
in a past life

Nice to see someone
who still likes doilies

Given away,
abandoned,
to have it's
story seen

I have tons at home
that my neighbours
don't want

More love to spread,
to share endlessly,
while looking back
through the holes

IT IS HERE

It is Here

It is here to grab you
It is here to snatch you
It is here to devour you

Drink your tears
For thirst
Stretch your tissues
For pleasure
Clog your throat
For silence

It is here to tangle you
It is here to strangle you
It is here to dangle you

Block your passions
Smash your clock

Laying on the bed
An image appears

A black figure
In front of a crimson red background
Hangs from a thick black noose
The body is at an acute angle

It flashes to zoom in
Into the pitch dark
Unknown faceless being

Thinking for a second
That you were
Going to be next

It is here

It is approaching you
Swiftly

It is an invisible gas
Ready

Hungry to feed upon your disbeliefs

Give it nothing
Keep your voice

And starve it
Before it starves you
Do you want the depths to starve you
Starve

CRIMSON RED

My mother said to me that I could pull off red

Crimson red, that was

Solid, smooth, silky red

Through the glass, I saw
A changing blush-pink face
Alive but pale

A shame the light
faded too soon

REALITY

As I got older
My colors started to fade
Stay colorful as you can be
For my creative mind is dying

It will take bullets
Take storms
Take time
Loudness
To get to where you want to be

Happy endings do not always exist

Some stories work out
A perfectly planned plot
Unlike non-fiction,
life is the opposite

There are always gonna be run-on sentences in someone's life

That is reality
We have to face
I am telling you
We die as we live

FINISH IT OFF

It's my turn
My turn
It's mine
Mine

It's your turn
Not
Getting down
Getting back up

I don't want to wear these
metallic accessories,
these chains no more

I collapse to my knees,
poorly waving my white flag

By the cliff of the field,
ready for my final mark

Finish me off,
and get the job done

Limbs aren't sturdy
Tissues are weak
Eyes almost closing

Finish me off,
what are you waiting for

I cherish my last breath

Take me out now
I'm slipping
Now is your chance

I'm clashing and crashing as
I break apart,
draining my energy in me
to where faith fades quickly

Tears of hopelessness
blur my vision

I'm not going anywhere
I'm going nowhere
Nowhere to go
All I can say is that I'm tired
And crying out

Finish me off

I plead for a sign of mercy
Sick of getting pushed
over and over
whenever I stand up

Finish me off

I'm throwing many beliefs in the trash
They say that there's a beginning
for every ending

I say for me,
there's a wall that awaits
at any moment that
I find myself in

I'm letting go

I'm not going anywhere
I'm going nowhere
Nowhere to go
Nowhere to go
All I can say is that I'm tired
Of this

Just when the end of me is nigh,
I grab my bow and arrow
Through bruises of words,
blisters of memories,
no instrument will pierce again

I lift myself up
with the last of my
remaining strength
Because I don't want to have myself saying

You win this round
I loose
You teared me down
I failed

Crumple me up fine like paper
Shatter me up good like glass

I will finish you off
And win this round
Look now
You will not finish me off
And tear me down

As I long as I

Don't let you crumple me up fine like paper
Won't let you shatter me up good like glass

Finish me off

My turn
Mine
My turn
It's mine
It's my turn
It's your turn
Not

Untouchable weapons slice through your thoughts

The soreness is gone

So go ahead
Do it already
And finish me off
Finish me off
I'm not giving up,
so I'll finish it off for you

ON AND ON

Carry on, carry on, my child, carry on
As the fighters are remembered by shining points
For the grand mountains
Be worn with red

As the sounds of roaring creatures fire their
Actions which devours a once

Home of life
As the souls of heroes discover what has been
Found that is a threat of control

Lead on, lead on, my child, lead on
These lives of who wish for a universe of love
Those who cherished Mother Nature's grain

The throne of us shall be within
Your spirit
The world of us shall be within
Your responsibility

For my blood vessels are filled with hypothermia's bite
And my heart is descending as each second of me washes by
What is yet to come may be unpredictable, but I have faith in you
You will find a way to bring on light
And dark
As one

My child, carry on, carry on, my child, lead on, lead on
For my end has come
My work here is done

Go on and on
And on

REALISM

My realism mourns
It's grieving and bleeding as
I will be alive

STILL SICK

I may still be sick

But I am homesick

Let me throw up

What I still have

From back home

SELFISH

There's a myth

Of how
suicide is selfish

It's false,
but one,
or some may
believe otherwise,

And that's
disappointing

No matter,
you can't change
someone's mindset so easily
when there are generation barriers

So if I, for one,
were to cut my own ties,
would you consider that selfish

Would you call me selfish
for feeling my pain

PROGRESSION

IF I'M BEING HONEST

If I can be viewed as valid,
my sleeves are soaking, soaking wet, wet with my exhausted
snots on my lavender sweater

That's if I'm being honest

I never trusted
Sharing my life's
Complications

That didn't deserve
to become
poisoning secrets

Who would've cared

If I can come forward,
with the negative thoughts that are raging within, the
controlled voices should gradually fade

STUPID POET

Not your average
stupid poet

I pity how nature
is spoken so highly,
spoken of being
so pretty,
too pretty,
too nice

Not in for profit,
we make
unlivable livings,
anyway

Ignorant contemporary art
is an insult that cloaks over
the gruesome realities

Stupid,
stupid,
stupid poet

Think of something
else or else

BURDEN

To my surprise,
you returned,
you didn't forget
about me

Took me in,
healed my blisters,
and spoke encouraging words
about me

None of you saw
the end of the world in me,
but praised my inner strength
and willingness to distant
myself from feeling like a burden,
because I never was

OVER MY DEAD BODY

It's over

Over my dead body
will I be taken
advantage of again

I may not be known
for keeping secrets
to the grave

Though I see
no trust to return,
and crossover

It's over

PITCH BLACK

We're not afraid of the dark anymore

Because we learned to live,
thrive off the darkness

Became hunters who attack
without warning

So when you're in the pitch black
Next time
Be on the lookout
We'll be there

THINK OF THE CABIN

Think of the cabin:
Handcrafted,
with mosaic glass installed

Think of the cabin
We will have
Once our dream succeeds

Think of the cabin
(though stay in the moment -
Adventures are to be lived now)

Out in New England's
Turquoise, raw green natures

Out in the home
Where we originated

A new story together
In a picture frame
Above the fireplace

Our lives will be beyond the borders

CANDLE BURNING

I know what it is
about the candle burning

Peaceful flame
whose desire rages

A yearning for hope,
a reason to feel

Hysteria-

A word so hard
for a build so destructible,
vulnerable

I know what this is-

Serenity

THE PLANE THAT RUNS IN THE FAMILY

The engine is passed down
and is either going to
roar or not be used at all

It gets broken,
it gets fixed

It stays grounded,
it flies high

That's the plane
that runs in
the family

Me,
I'm going to travel
this world

Unwelcome or not

HOW TO MAKE WISHES OUT OF DANDELIONS

They're someone
who I can't have

There's someone
who I don't reach

The level of success they possess,
surpasses me, a commoner

Out of the crowd
that reeks with desperation,
I stand in my place
because I learned
how to make wishes
out of dandelions

And my wish for them
is to be content

Whether I'm there or not in their life

ESTATE SALE

A home is left behind

Your pictures of the trips you've taken,
your favorite blankets and pillows on your bed,
your decorations and awards you've shown guests,
your clothes and treasures tucked away

Your livelihood,
gone

Within a day,
your life becomes
an estate sale

And all you can
bring to the after life
are your memories
and the quality
of your soul

GARDENS

If all else fails, dear,
reflect back on your first home
where your dreams started

Give yourself the chance
to discover further dreams
since the roots stand still

Remember the gardens you make

NEW NORMAL

Knowing
I

Will or may
Not feel or be

Who I
Was before,
is a loss hope,
is this the new normal

Media crushed
my stagnated dreams

However, as another chapter comes around,
anew, I am born ev'ryday

HUES

There is the love
Of a friend

And there is the love
Of a family

How can you love another
If you cannot love yourself

How can you take care another
If you cannot take care of yourself before them

Nobody should care who you embrace
Who you love
Sincere love is flourished love

And hate is angered
Love's misunderstood and confused friend
Angered that you have a found and fond
Love so vibrant, feelings so brilliant

Exhilaration
Drowns out the oppressors' wish

Hate subconsciously craves attention
Gives the aggressors
Further ideas to destroy
Feed their fuming desire
All for nothing
Their love wasted

The heartless want builded pressure
Order
Enough to break
What they want to erase from you

Why be ashamed
For their foolish actions

I do love you
For you

Do you love you
For you

I respect you for who you are
Love you for you

We did not ask for anything
And yet we had the chance to love

Could there be a better feeling
Than being loved
Reunited
Cared for

We have a chance to love
With all hues of love
When we are ready to
You have the chance to
Love your hues
More than I will do

BLUE LENS

When I thought blue lens
were the only way I
could see the world
and my life,
my despair was finally
lifted off my aching shoulders

Developed clarity,
encouraged strength,
from my particularly blind eyes

Helped me

With a
discarded canvas and
explored shades of

White

Purple

Pink

Brown

Orange

Red

Yellow

Black

Green

Grey

Colors
Feelings
Expressions

To feel
with a sense to regain
lost pigments

Through a distorted mind,
I can see
and feel
more colors
again

BEING IS BEING

Never apologize for being human
Nor regret singing your own name

What is the point
Express yourself

Pour out the emotions you feel
In which pull you down

A tiny feeling can be as little as a pebble
In your shoe
Or carry a sack of boulders on your back

Anything can be a chip on your shoulder
That you are just waiting to flick off
And then to start itching off the sense of the previous presence
Again

Secrets
Stories
News

Horrific or terrific events

The desperate urge to get that energy off one's chest is painful
It may be exciting to suck in it before blurbing it all out

Truth and guilt

It is a cycle to soak in
For you

And another
Or more

Any deal can mean differently or personally
Depending on their

Thoughts
Experiences
Surroundings

Someone in the world wants to
And will value your inner voice

Drink your glass of liquefied time each day
Just do not chug it all at once

Believe me
I was thirsty as well

There is always a day and a night
Though not like today and tomorrow

Feel majestic

Feel majestic for crying on your pillow after a situation
For caring for someone
Love be forbidden or not

People are born to seek, spread, and share affection
Some conclusions
Do not end as well as others

We are breathing to have crimson and clear liquid drip
We are alive to naturally
Develop temptations

No need to hideaway
The shameful shadows you wish to vanish

Feel free to reveal your hidden truthful emotions
Behind any manipulative mask

It is all a part of being beautifully biotic
Being is being

The process of experiencing
All organisms are born
Genetically designed or natured

Then formed and forced
Under certain circumstances

When you get

Embarrassed
Or feel invincible

In this reality
We are here

To hear
To see
To touch
To smell
To taste

In order to discover
Define the world ourselves
If only someone could feel the texture of your memories
A living you
Within the life of nature

WORD FOR WORD

Be wary

For me

Living in the moment is a task than a simple deep breath
A task in which I attempt to complete
If I catch my restless brain acting up a scene

I will get there

The pathway was not very established, it was more of a field
A field of average cut grass

To explore and find a name for myself
Searching for a reason, just one meaning behind my identity
The visual, the title doesn't come around that easily, that expectedly

When will I get there

Well, where is where and where is there
Are the two unproportional arms going to tell me when

To step back to base must be a relief, to avoid collision in a step ahead
As much as I desire for the entrance, to learn how to move at a fulfilling pace

Leads to a life living word for word
The course will pass on this rock

While I gather the presents
I earned out of my efforts

I will sure to be humble, to cherish these grateful scenes

I will reach out while I run

PARTY HARD

I don't like to party hard,
not so much of a college-goer,
you know
what I mean

Tonight
I was reminded
of what it meant
to be young

Thanks to the music
Thanks to the people

I remembered how to dance

All eyes were on me
as my safe shell broke
one beat at a time

CONFESSION

I was around three years old
when my great grandparents
gifted me a grand bureau
with a mirror

A part of a full set of luxury

Recently, I chipped off one of the wooden bureau's
knobs

And once I threw
my plastic hair brush,
powered by a sudden strike of fuming anger

The dismembered pencils on the bed watched me do
it, too

What have I done

A BLESSED CURSE OR A CURSED BLESSING

Is it a gift? Some passion which you so coincidentally had
naturally?
Did it find you or did you find it?

What if a gift gifted itself to you
Or multiple gifts gifted the same gift to you

Without a "to and from" tag on it
Without a wrap of paper or even a ribbon or bow on it
It's not in a box, it's simply there by you and bare

Would you accept it
Even if it could possibly mean the worse
But the worse could be for the better
Even if it could possibly mean the better
But the better could be for the worse
If you never cared nor if you knew
Would you still risk the chances and let it guide you
To define the mysterious and the unknown
Whether it be the journey or who you are

I remember one of my gifts, I do
It found me and now I'm letting it lead me to destiny, but soon
enough for me
I'm gonna have to lead it to every person, just like how their gift
did so to them

Call a gift whatever, whether you think it may be
A blessed curse or a cursed blessing
But it's a gift, so take it or leave it to make something positive out
of it

Your perspective can define your reality and you can choose your surroundings

Would you think that the Sun was rising or setting in a still life

painting

THANK YOU

As human, thank you, you sculpted the person who I am today
As human, thank you, you made me feel like I was made less

You stared at me
in doubt of everything

I appreciate how you used to never see me as anything
That's how you made me think that I was nothing

Thank you

Thank you, you gave me the power that dominates yours
Thank you, you discriminated me and my passions

You didn't value me
because of my status

I appreciate how you considered me to be an outsider
That's how you made me believe that I was not important

Thank you

Thank you
Is all that I have to say

And I thought I was the one
who should have been
ashamed of themselves

BETTER THINGS TO DO

These two decades
Of torture
Have gotten old
I'm past
The pain

I've got better things to do

Than to waste potential

My potential

DIFFERENTLY EXTRAORDINARY

I am one
with the colors
and numbers

Of currents
that swirl
and make
the sea

I splash
in glee
in a
school
of diverse
beings

I accept
the natural
functions of
my entirety

For the
shallow minded
who cannot
come to terms
with acceptance,
they have my sympathy,
but never my obligations

My senses carry me,
I am not suffering

I am living

I am as different,
differently
extraordinary

As any human

THE FIRST

You are
the first

To have reached
a milestone,
which required
determination
and motivation

Led by a
celebration
that calls
to honor
and highlight
the generation
of graduation

The accomplished
privilege
that will shed
a brighter light
on your aspirations

CREATIVITY

You cannot force
creativity,
of course

Do not dare to
focus on what
the product
should be

Picture your art
of what it is
meant to be

HER AURA

Enriched,
she welcomed a cool gust of plant life,
after a hike well worth living through

Enchanted,
her aura beamed upon the dreadful dead,
thus a whole new reason for green bloomed

Enabled,
the lands were under her command,
now that there's growth to improve

The sprouting, artistic aspirations

WHERE THE LIGHT IS COMING FROM

All that's best,
all I want you to do
is see that we're all
unique flowers
in the same soil

And I hope at least you
will see that because some
don't know where the light
is coming from

STRING OF LIGHTS

My
inner being
is warmed
by a
string
of
lights

Little bulbs
I see
hold the past
of
friendship-hood

Aglow,
it goes
and
gifts me
bits of
their
sparkling
joy

UNDER MY UMBRELLA...

Stand under my umbrella...
For I
Will shelter you

Be under my umbrella...
For I
Will be there for you

Whenever you're in the blue
Or
In the colorless world

Run under my umbrella...
For I
Will guide you

Go under my umbrella...
For I
Will protect you

Whether you're lost
Or
In a dark nightmare

Under my umbrella
You'll be safe
Here with
Me

THE YOU

For those who need it

Why is your symbol on the concrete
No need to be ashamed
Embrace the braces
Adore the acne

I'm a misfit

Every bit of detail
Makes you
The you
That you are
You are unique
But who are you now

To me you were
The definition of confidence
But you ran
You ran away beyond the meadows
Oh, wherever did you go

Not far

In all honesty
Perfection should not be
A first priority
Do not make yourself up with the other makeup
You glow just as much without the changes
I am here

Pick up your wand
You will lose your magic
I can see that you
Want to have the rain
Camouflage Niagara Falls

I'll face away, but I won't run

But who does not
Look fearful when they are yanked by the neck
Be careful of drowning in your own stream
Even I fall at times
When the thoughts hit me

Are those the ones
The reason why you are
Not wearing your smile
Darling don does not have them
Dull your natural shine
They feed upon negativity
Nevertheless, I will stay
They will remain

Inhale

Why now

Exhale

What's your point

Not all stories have an unhappy ending
This may just be the beginning
That's a challenge to overcome

Inhale

Trying

Exhale

I can barely breathe

I will stay in your cold
And remain in this storm
And conquer these winds with you

My sugar cube
Reality made you
To be human
Bittered you up
Not to be perfect

Stay true to yourself
Why be anybody else
When you were destined to evolve

You know better
Than to let the skeletons and organs stumble in

And you know that
I love
The you
That you are

But

Regardless of your quirks and flaws
As said as before
And it is no lie in disguise

I love
The you
That you are

I love the you that you are

You are the disgusting grace of nature
And the perfect to me
Wear your symbol with pride

And stand a little taller for me
For you are the remaining light
Peering through the cracked boulders
That is you
The you

APOLOGIZE

Never apologize for being human

You're saying sorry
For things that aren't your fault
Who or what are you protecting?
Your reputation, perhaps, image

What made you into whom?
And who made you into what?

Designed to have red and clear liquid drip
Alive to naturally develop temptations

No need to hide away
The shameful shadows
You wish to vanish

Feel free to reveal
Your hidden truths
Behind the manipulative mask

It's all
About
Being beautifully biotic

A SMILE

A smile comes from a person's heart strings, not their words
A smile comes from a person's pleasure, not their voice

You help fade my stress away and my frown
And you always make my blue cloud upside down

A smile is the cure for any sad emotion
A smile is the cure to anyone's paused motion

You are my smile, that I wear every day

A seed comes from a person's dreams, not their imagination
A seed comes from a person's mind, not their life

You help me write my wishes and my plans
And you always make my ideas become a piece of land

A seed is the cure for any poor dear
A seed is the cure to somebody's cheer

You are my seed, that I plant every day

A light comes from a person's acceptance, not their mood
A light comes from a person's generosity, not their gift

You help me go towards the right path
And to avoid me from all the wrath

A light is the cure for a new day
A light is the cure to be shared, if you may

You are my light, that I see everyday

A book comes from a person's experience, not their view
A book comes from a person's art, not their sight

You help me get another adventure
And to take in another world

A book is the cure for a human's soul
A book is the cure to achieve a goal

You are my book, that I read everyday

A butterfly comes from a person's smile, not their purity
A butterfly comes from a person's seed, not their interest

They got help by friends and family on their journey
And was taught subjects that they never knew was true

A butterfly comes from a person's lifetime, not their timeline
A butterfly comes from a person's idea, not their thinking

I need a bright light before I trip over my dreams
I need a good book before I lose all of my hope

I am a butterfly, everyday

HOLD MY HAND TIGHT

Take me away
Rock me to sleep
Drift me far and far

Hug me from all
Silence out that noise
Hold my hand tight
Tell me that I'm alright

Have me escape
On the tower's walls
Hold my hand tight
Assure me that it's ok

Give me a home
Block the Sun and Moon
Watch me as I go

Kill life's light
Tone down death's sight
Lift me higher

And dare me to look down

Carry my candle
Towards the hope

Please

Because if we let go
Of one another

We'll collapse

Take me away
Give me a home
Carry my candle

Please
Please
Please

Please

Please

LOVE'S PERSONIFICATION

Love comes in all different shapes and sizes

Love has no face
Love has no body
Love has no template

There's no question
in love's personification

Love has voices
Love has spectrums
Love has meanings

Love appears in all different shades and spirits

The mightiest aura
that gravitates beings
such as us

ASTRONOMICAL TEMPLE

Wherever you are,
you are not far

Constellations collide,
interrupting the quiet,
regaining stolen voices

An astronomical temple
we call home

Where laws
are not defined
by grammar
and unwritten rules

THE FREE

You are
the free

To progress
your knowledge,
to express
your identity

After you throw
your cap
in the air,
and enter
the world

This time,
with experience
behind your back

You are
the educated
who will change,
who will challenge
that world
where hate is
easier than love

For hate is colorless,
but pinches your nose
from its distinctive odor

Fly out of

the nest

Towards the
flock of
dreaming birds
Iron Lung

Cast a hug,
embrace me whole
around my defenceless body

You said you would,
would be there
until my very end
with you

Your iron long cocooned
me,
and you,
you said you would be there

You were, all this time
to keep me
well and alive

BELOVED PARTNER

Beloved partner
of mine
has moved on
to the other side

They wanted me to not
be alone for the
rest of my life

Here I am, back in the wild

Here you are, startled by my encounter

You almost poked and pinned me

Remember how
your eyes widened

When we first met,
how were either of us to know,
we'd be lovers
making history

FEBRUARY

For the first time in February,
the short tempered month,
full of vicious frost bites
over a course of decades

I'm not born again in a blizzard
I'm reborn in refreshing winds

Where the rain cries
for better weather

ANIMATED CADAVER

Stitch the wounds back up
with rusted orchestral strings
from my unmarked grave

FRESHEST BLOOD

Mine for the roughest diamond
to test under pressure

Hunt for the freshest blood
there is out there

The torch is aflame
enough to pass on
to a worthy candidate

DEAD NAME

A new being
I'm not

My dead name
was never a part
of my identity

No name,
stage name,
pen name,
real name,
is

It tells stories instead

Stories to write out
more parts of you

That's what makes you,
you

BEST OF THE BEST

Sure,
I'm from the boonies,
and I'm proud of my heritage

Left my origins to stand
along my relaxed coffin,
before fields and bridges

To earn my respect,
as competition
isn't solely a match

Against the best of the best

A dream since childhood,
I will be a hexed elite
in the brightest city
among a prestigious team
of the best
of the best

That will be me
This will be us
The best of the best

CAY WITH A "C"

There's a stage
after stage
to not only
perform,
but to
live on

People of
all ages,
thanks to
viewers like
you,
we proudly present

Cay,
Cay with a "C"

WHATEVER

Call me whatever,
but don't say
that I'm "whatever"

OVERNIGHT

Cradled by the blood moon

A dream is dreamt overnight

Unlike a dreamed reality

Sleep tightly

CITY STREETS

Once I return with my
harnessed abilities

I'll show the city streets
the songs I've written

Only this time around,
the people will be quiet

And I'm
getting
alarmingly
stronger

ONE MORE ENCORE

Too many dreams
are running free
as I travel and meet
places, people upon regions

My mind expands,
makes more room for life

Didn't believe I'd get to live
this much and this far
in and of my life

I could do
one more encore,
call for a new tour,
and let the event,
the story
happen

WHICH ONE IS NOT LIKE THE OTHER

Traveling through the chaotic crowd
Hundreds, or maybe even thousands of others
Are moving the streets
None of which, were aglow

Expect one if you played which one is not like the other

This one skipped
While the others walked
This one jumped
While the others stomped

That one was just all in it for the thrill of the world

This one laughed
While the others yelled
This one smiled
While the others grinned

While the others looked straight ahead
They never dared to look a little higher
Like no other, they did

ABOUT THE AUTHOR

Cay

Cay (Kayla Pellegrini) is a newly established poet and writer. From their hometown of Concord, New Hampshire, Cay tripped in love with writing at Christa McAuliffe School in 5th grade. Following then, they started writing simple poems throughout their time at Rundlett Middle School. Cay also began songwriting music and lyrics, which went hand-in-hand with their poetry.

Sometime after Concord High School as a 2020 graduate, their poetry has been featured in the Cape Fear Voices and The Teen Scene, a local newspaper. They also wrote articles for Leland Magazine and Southport Magazine for freelance writing. On their own time, they post their poetry and videos of themselves reciting their work on multiple social media platforms. Cay currently resides in New York, New York with their pet betta fish, Cherry.

Cay enjoys various genres and styles and loves to experiment with creative writing. Literature and the arts were never-ending forms of self-expression for Cay. They hope you, the spectator, receive representation and recognition from their poetry. Cay thanks you, since Earth is inhabited by choas. There are wordless and imageless words that are yet to be investigated.

So write like crazy.

Rhetoric Maniac
Cay

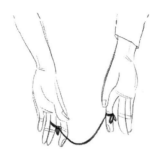

Made in the USA
Columbia, SC
21 June 2022

61967096R00150